My Childhood Inspirations The Series
Book 1:
Little Girl

by

Joyce Green

Copyright © 2015 by Joyce Green

All rights reserved. This book or any portion thereof may not be reproduced or used in any manner whatsoever without the express written permission of the author and/or publisher except for the use of brief quotations in a book review.

Illustrator: Jucalstudios@gmail.com

Publisher: G Publishing LLC

ISBN: 978-0-9969684-0-9

Library of Congress Control Number: 2015920431

Published and Printed in the United States of America

Warm Acknowledgements to my Grandchildren
for Ideas and Insights!

Sequoyeth Simpson

Sheyenne Simpson

Shaydon Simpson

I wrote these true stories for my grandchildren.

Where I Got My Name

Holding My Breath

My First BF (Best Friend)

Grits and Green Split-Pea Soup

Happiness

Ma's Top of the Stove Cast-Iron Cornbread

Where I Got my Name!

"Ma …. MA … MAAAA!!!" I yelled, as I burst through the torn screen door onto the porch.

It was late May on Long Island, New York. There was a little nippy breeze gently blowing across the front porch that morning. The sun was rising and a bunch of crows and sparrows were in the trees, singing away.

The smell of purple flowers on the lilac tree in the backyard filled the air. Ma was sitting in her favorite chair next to a big green ivy plant, reading the newspaper, looking for coupons and what was on sale.

"MA-A!" I shouted.

Ma kept her head down. She continued reading the newspaper.

"Maaaa, are you listening to me?" I asked.

Ma just kept on reading the paper.

I waited. Then, "Ma … ma," I said softly.

Finally, Ma slowly raised her head and looked at me. "I heard you," she said. "Stop yelling."

I should have known better than to shout at Ma. "Where did my name come from?" I asked softly.

I pulled a little old chair near Ma and sat. Ma put the paper down and looked at me with a serious expression on her face.

Gently, I asked again, "Ma, where did my name come from?"

"The wind," she said.

"The *wind!*"

Ma gazed at me disapprovingly.

"Sorry," I said. I had yelled again…

Then I asked again, more quietly, "The wind?"

"Yes," she said, "the wind named you."

"But—you and Daddy gave me my name, right?" I asked.

"Your Daddy and other folks in the family named most of our children, but I heard your name in the wind," she explained.

"You did?" I asked excitedly.

"Yes, I did," she said.

"What did the wind say to you?" I asked.

That's when Ma told me the story of "How I Got My Name!"

Ma began, "One cloudy day, in October or early November, I was in the backyard taking clothes off the clothesline.

It had been a sunny day, but, that afternoon, some big rain clouds rolled into the sky. Now, I was pregnant and had been carrying you in my stomach for about seven months.

My belly was real big, so I was waddling around like a duck, in the backyard. I knew it was gonna rain, so I tried to hurry up because it was cold out there too."

It was so cold the clothes on the clothesline were half frozen. I took the half-frozen clothes off the clothesline, put them in a clothes basket, carried them into the house, and emptied the clothes basket on top of the washing machine. I went back out the door to get the rest of the clothes off the second clothesline.

The wind started blowin' hard. I was standing outside the door, on the back stoop, holding the empty clothes basket. After I put the last frozen shirt in the clothes basket, I dropped some of the wooden clothespins in the basket.

All of a sudden, a big blast of wind came up and blew my dress up my legs. I dropped the clothes basket and some of the clothes fell out on the ground. *Oooh*, that wind was *sooooo* cold I got chill bumps. Then, the wind began blowing and howling. Big rain drops splashed on my face. I got a little nervous.

I wrapped my little coat around me and squatted down on the ground to pick up the clothes that had fallen out the basket. Then I heard this kinda wailing sound. It was like a whisper—'….ooy..se….oooy .se…'"

Listening to Ma's story, I felt as if I were in a trance.

"I looked around," Ma continued. "What was that? It sounded like the wind was talking—saying

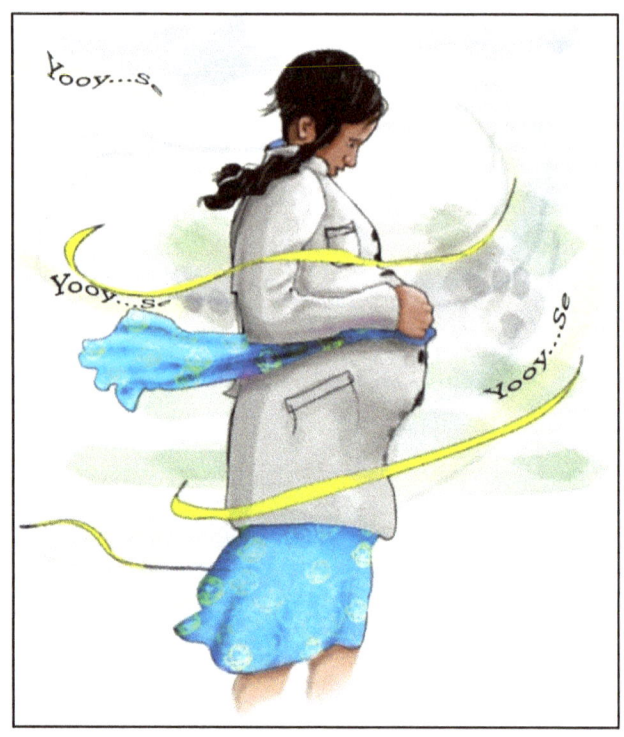

'Yoooy..se, Yooy ce…' Then you made a big kick in my stomach… two times. Just like you heard the wind call you.

My eyes got real big, and my heart started pounding real hard.

I grabbed the clothes and went waddling into the house as fast as I could. After I closed the door and felt safe, I peeked out the window and looked into the backyard.

It was raining. A stray dog trotted through the backyard sniffing around at the bottom of some trees. The dog made its way through the back path to the next house.

That night, I told your Daddy what happened when I was taking the clothes off the clothesline. He looked at me and grinned. Your Daddy never had much to say about things.

I told him, 'If this baby is a girl, I want to name her 'Joyce' because I heard that name in the wind.' I thought that name was given to me.

I don't know if he believed me, but he laughed and said, 'Okay, okay—but only if it's a girl.'

When you were born, you were small and baldheaded. You were different than the other children because you were frail and a little sickly. But you were a very soft and sensitive baby. So I took your name from what I thought I heard in the wind. I named you 'Joyce.'"

I smiled at Ma with deep affection and delight. I thought, *I will always remember how I got my name from the wind and be proud of it!*

Holding My Breath

I heard Momma and Daddy in the kitchen talking real loud to each other. I think they were mad about something. I was in my crib in the bedroom. The bedroom was next to the kitchen.

I wanted to get out of that crib. I had made a BIG "do-do" in my diaper, and it was real wet. So I started crying… real loud. But Daddy and Mommy kept on talking real loud to each other.

My brothers and sister were used to Mommy and Daddy talking loud to each other. They didn't like it. But sometimes *they* shouted at each other too.

Mommy and Daddy didn't talk to each other real loud much, but my three brothers and sister did it all the time. When any of them did it, the noise and their loud talking made me cry and get nervous.

On this day, Daddy and Mommy were talking loud about fixing the back stoop. Mommy wanted another bathroom in our house. We had only one bathroom upstairs, and seven people in the house: five children and Mommy and Daddy. There were a lot of us.

I stood in my crib, trembling. I started to shake my head back and forth to make the noise go away. But, the noise and yelling kept getting louder. Mommy heard me crying and came into the bedroom where I was, all the while still fussing at Daddy.

Mommy saw by my expression that I was in distress. I was sweating and trying hard to catch my breath. I couldn't. So I held my breath instead.

The next thing I remember, I was sitting on Mommy's lap, and Mommy was blowing air in my face. Daddy was standing over Mommy, staring at me.

I looked at Mommy and started to cry. She patted me on the back and rocked me for a little while.

Then Mommy said, "Go to your Daddy," and handed me to Daddy.

Well … Daddy was totally confused about what happened to me.

I grabbed one of Mommy's hair braids as tight as I could. I didn't want to go to that Daddy. I wanted to stay with Mommy instead of going to that mean Daddy.

I was out of luck. Mommy plopped me on Daddy's chest. Daddy grabbed me. Then Mommy went back to the kitchen.

Well, did I ever holla! I looked at that Daddy. He looked mean. *Holla! .... holla! ….* I kept twisting around, looking for my mommy.

Daddy sighed, then held me up high in the air, with two hands. I was hollering and crying ... Then that Daddy brought me down closer to his face. His face and nose were real close to my face and my nose.

Daddy stared me in the face for a long time. I was still hollering. Then he said, real deep and low, "Stop it!" *Ooh*, my eyes got big, and I started to holler even louder.

I turned my head to the door to find Mommy. That Daddy turned my whole body around so that I was looking him straight in the eyes again. "Stop that," he said; "be quiet."

Well, I was terrified. I began to whimper. I still looked for Mommy, but she stayed in the kitchen. Daddy pulled me close. As he held me, again he said, "Be quiet"—and I was.

Then that Daddy put me on his shoulder. It's hard to remember exactly, but he carried me over to a bedroom window. Daddy and me stared out the window for a long time. We watched the birds fly in and out of the apple tree. Then a squirrel ran up our chestnut tree. I had calmed down by then.

Soon Daddy took me into the kitchen and handed me back to Mommy.

I grabbed Mommy and held on tight. I peeked over her shoulder at that Daddy. He looked at me and walked away.

Daddy left the kitchen and came back with tools and started fixing the back stoop.

After that day, Daddy and Mommy did fuss less with each other because I really got upset when they fussed or argued. It made me feel like screaming, and I would start gasping, taking short breaths.

Whenever Mommy and Daddy would start to fuss, Mommy would look at me.

Sometimes I would cover my ears to block out the sound of their voices. When Mommy saw me do that or fidget, Mommy would tell Daddy, "Stop, stop! The baby's gonna faint or something." Mommy would come running and get me. Daddy would be right behind her. Ma would lay me over her knees on my stomach, pat my back, and sort of bounce me up and down.

When I had calmed down considerably and was merely sniffling, Daddy would grab me and hold me—my squinted-up face to his face—and tell me, "Stop." I would stop.

Eventually, whenever Mommy and Daddy wanted to fuss, they would first look to see where I was. If I was around, they would just mumble and roll their eyes at each other, then quiet down.

When I got older, Ma told me how I would hold my breath and faint if she and Daddy fussed and argued.

"You used to scare us," she said, laughingly, "but, when we started to argue, we stopped because we knew it might upset you and even the other children."

I still remember that when Daddy got me, I had better do what he said. I could get away with crying to get my way with Mommy, but—my Daddy ... NO!

My First BF (Best Friend)

Ma washed clothes every day early in the morning. Then she hung the clothes on the clothesline with wooden clothespins so that the sun would dry them.

Ma always made sure we all were dressed and fed. Then, "Go outside," she'd tell us while Daddy left for work.

We would be outside all day except when we came in to eat lunch. So I was free to go play with my best friend (bf), Gail, on the next block, behind our house at the half-a–house, our special meeting place.

The half-a-house was really a big hole in the ground where home builders had laid a cement foundation for a new house's cellar.

It had a wooden floor built on top of the cement foundation.

But then the builders abandoned the house.

The half-a-house was right behind Gail's Grandpa's house, where Gail and her brother lived. On the other side of the half a house lived Alfonso, my oldest brother's best friend. Gail and I liked the half-a-house because it had a lot of sand and dirt around it to play in. We played in that dirt and sand a few hours every day. It was fun to play there because nobody would bother us.

And it was better than going over to Gail's house.

One morning I went over to Gail's house and knocked on the door. Gail's Grandpa answered the door. I was real scared. He was so tall he looked like a giant—a giant with squinty eyes. He had a lot of white in his hair, and he was real big and real brown.

"Can Gail come out to play?" I asked, backing up real fast. I saw Gail peeking out through the little glass window on the side of the door.

"GAIL IS BUSY; GO HOME!" he said, real loud and gruff.

Did I ever! I tore off, running home with tears in my eyes.

I stayed away from Gail's house from then on, because her Grandpa was so big and mean. So it was better for us to meet at the half-a-house.

Even though I was only around five or six years old, Ma allowed me to go through the back path behind our house to the half-a-house and play with Gail. From our backyard, Ma could pretty much keep an eye on us, and I could always hear her if she called me.

Of course, it seemed as if *everyone* was keeping an eye on us then. My brother's friend Al and his sister, who lived next door to the half-a-house, were always outside in their yard. I thought they were *sooo* nosey because they were always watching us.

In our neighborhood, someone was always watching what was going on, especially that little old White lady who lived in the house behind ours. She used to sit outside on her porch, just watching.

Almost every day I would take the path behind our house to meet Gail at the half-a-house. I had to go past that White lady's house. As usual, there she was, sitting on her porch, watching me as I ran past her house to meet Gail.

Back then, everybody knew who lived in the neighborhood. People's doors were always unlocked. Even at night you could sleep in your house with your screen door closed—hardly ever locked. You even could sleep on your porch at night if you wanted to. Most people didn't have fans, so, if it was hot, they would go outside and sit on their porches or sit in the shade under the trees.

I ran to the half-a-house. There was Gail, playing in the sand. Without saying a word, I kneeled down and started playing in the dirt too. I found a stick on the ground. The dirt was real hard, so I had to use two hands and my stick to get the dirt loose.

The stick broke, so I found another stick that was bigger and stronger. I piled some loose sand and dirt near Gail's pile of sand and dirt.

"What are you doing?" I asked Gail.

"I'm making pies," she said.

"Oh," I said. "What kind of pies?"

"All kinds," she said. Gail gave me a kind of "duh!" look, then went back to stirring the dirt she had piled up.

Using my stick, I started stirring up my dirt pile. I wanted to make pies too.

"How we gonna mix up our pies?" Gail asked me. Then she answered her own question: "We need a bowl," she said.

"And some water," I shouted. "I know where a bowl is!"

"Where?" she asked.

"At my house," I said.

"You gonna get it?" she asked.

"Yeah," I said. "Let's go!"

We ran past the little old White lady's house. She was still sitting on her porch. We looked at her. She looked at us. We kept on running through the back path to my backyard. I ran up the three steps to the back door. Gail followed me to the steps, but she stayed outside. I went in to the house to get a bowl.

The coast was clear; Ma was upstairs. I looked

under the sink where Ma kept a lot of bowls. I pulled out a big shiny one. I was in such a hurry to get back outside before Ma came downstairs that I left the cabinet door under the sink open.

I took the bowl and ran back outside. Then Gail and I, both holding the big bowl, loped through the back path, back to the half-a-house. Guess who was sitting on the porch watching ... Yeah, you guessed it: that little old White lady! She looked real scary that day. It was summertime, but she was all bundled up in winter clothes. She asked, "What you-all doing with that bowl?"

My eyes got real big. "Uh-oh," I said. *She's gonna tell on us*, I thought. Gail dropped her end of the bowl and ran to the half-a-house for safety. The bowl hit the side of my left leg real hard, and it hurt.

Without saying a word to that old White lady, I dragged the bowl over to the half-a-house.

"Why did you leave me?" I screamed at Gail.

"I'm scared of that lady," she said.

"She's not gonna bother you," I said.

"She looks scary," Gail said.

"Help me," I urged her as I dragged the bowl to the three mounds of dirt and sand Gail and I had piled up. She did.

We began putting the dirt and sand in the bowl with a stick, but the sticks were too narrow to make good spoons. So we used our hands. "Yuk," I mumbled. There were a lot of little rocks and crawly things in that dirt.

When the bowl was half-full of sand and dirt, we stopped. "We need some water to mix up our pies," Gail said.

"You can get some water from your house," I said to Gail. "Your house is right there."

"Oh no, I can't," said Gail, "My Grandpa would make me come in the house if he saw me at the water hose."

"Okay," I sighed, "I got some water at my house. We can make pies at my house."

"Yaaay," Gail said, and we left the half-a-house, dragging the half-full shiny bowl of dirt and sand to the back path past that old White lady's porch. Gail was peeking to see where the old White lady was. She had gone inside.

Gail and I both grabbed an end of the bowl and carried it to my backyard. In my backyard, a broken sidewalk led to our beat-up garage.

On the cement floor inside the garage was a dirty plastic cup. I ran into the garage, got that dirty old plastic cup, and—while Gail looked for a new stirring stick—ran around the back hedges to the spigot on the side of my house so we could get the water we needed to stir up our pies.

The handle on the water spigot was metal and shaped like a four-leaf clover, and it was very hard to turn. I used both hands and all my might to open that spigot. The water barely came out in a dribble. I got only a little water in my cup.

I better try again, I thought. I put my hands back

on the spigot, shut my eyes, and, with all my strength, I tried to turn the spigot handle. "OOOOh!" I screeched.

The water burst out of the spigot. Water drenched my face, hair, top, shorts, and sneakers.

"Hurry up!" called Gail. "I'm ready to mix it."

Half wet, I left the water running, got the plastic cup, filled it up, and ran around the hedges back to where Gail was squatting. She looked at me and said, "OoOoo—you're all wet. Your momma's gonna get you!"

"No she's not," I said hotly. I stood there and poured the water from the cup into the bowl.

"Stop, STOP!!" she yelled. "You're wetting me."

And, I was... Gail was squatting next to the bowl and had been laughing at me, so I splashed the water in the cup all over her. The water splashed the dirt and sand in the bowl—and her top, pants, and shoes too. I even got some mud on my pants and sneakers. Now we were both equally messy.

But Gail and I were lucky. Because it was a hot summer day, our clothes got warm and began to dry quickly. I watched Gail mix the dirt, sand, and water until it was too thick to stir anymore. "It's too hard to turn," she said. She looked at me, and I looked at her. We looked at each other and that mud bowl for what seemed like a long time.

Since it was a hot day, the bowl and mud in it began to warm up. "If we're gonna make pies, we gotta touch it," I said.

"You touch it," Gail said.

"You touch it first." I said.

I looked at the bowl. Gail had already laughed at me for being wet, soooooo ...I timidly touched the top of the mud in the bowl. "It's warm," I squealed; "it's warm!" I got a little braver and picked up a handful of warm mud. I began squeezing and patting the mud into patties. Gail looked at me and dug her hands into the mud.

We began making patties at warp speed. Boy, were we busy. All along the edge of the cracked sidewalk, we were lining up pies that looked like little brown cookies with chips (stones) in them. Then we decided to make some pies bigger, just like Ma made. Now our pies were the size of big saucers.

By now, we had mud all over our hands, arms, legs, and sneakers. We were wet and warm, but we kept on making our pies. All of a sudden we heard my Ma calling.

"Joyce! JOOY..CE!" Ma yelled. I heard her, and I knew, from the sound of her voice, that I was in big trouble. But my best friend, Gail, and I were cooking! We were in the backyard making the prettiest mud pies you ever saw.

Gail's eyes got real big when she heard Ma's voice. It was real scary—and Gail was real scared. That's when she suddenly remembered that she had come over to my house without asking her Grandpa's permission. She turned around to go back through the path and—guess who was standing across the street looking for her.... You guessed it: that mean old GRANDPA!!!!

Meanwhile, Ma came to the back door. She opened the door, looked at me and saw Gail running through the path to go home. Then Ma saw Gail's

Grandpa. She waved at Gail's Grandpa as Gail ran across the street to him.

"Bring my bowl back into this house this minute!" Ma shouted. Now I got scared. I knew I was in for it. I was shaking, and my feelings were hurt!. Why was everybody yelling and looking so mean? Why was Ma so angry?

Ma saw the puzzled look on my face. She saw the tears welling up in my eyes. She quickly calmed down and said, "Come over here. You look a mess. Look at all that mud on your clothes. Look at your face and wet hair."

With tears on my cheeks, I dragged the muddy bowl over to Ma. Ma shook her head. "Mmm .... mmm".. she mumbled. Then she said, "You better be glad this bowl is okay. Now come with me to the side of the house. We have to wash the mud out this bowl."

I followed Ma to the water spigot. She wasn't happy that I'd left the water running all this time. But she didn't say anything (her look said it all).

She adjusted the water flow and rinsed the bowl out. Then she cupped her hands together and made a little bowl under the leaking spigot.

When her hands were almost full of water, she threw the cold water on me. She got real tickled when she saw the expression on my tear-stained face. My eyes got big and I cried harder. *That's not funny*, I thought.

Ma laughed and grabbed my hand. We went inside the house. I had to leave all my clothes and my sneakers in the back room near the washing machine. Then Ma gave me a bath.

Ma asked, "Little Gail is your friend?"

"Yes, my best friend," I replied.

Ma asked, "Where is she now?"

"She ran home 'cause she heard your voice and knew we were in big trouble." I said. "An' her mean old Grandpa was standing right there at the half-a-house."

"Now you in trouble all by yourself," Ma said. "Sometimes friends want you to do what they don't want to do" Ma said.

"Why?" I asked, really confused.

"Because they know that they will get in trouble if they do it. So some friends will tell *you* to do it. That way, if you get in trouble, they won't."

That was the only time Gail came over to my house. After maybe two weeks or so, I saw Gail at the half-a-house, and we played in the sand and dirt a few more times. But eventually she stopped coming there. Soon, Gail left her Grandpa's house for good, even though her brother stayed there a while longer.

Time passed. The next summer I went over to the half-a-house to play in the sand and dirt by myself.

It was different now. I was playing alone without my friend Gail. After a while, I stopped going to the half-a-house.

Even though a lot of people lived in my house, they were all older than me. Nobody was like my best friend, Gail. Years later, my brother told me that Gail's mom had come and got her. They moved to California. I missed my friend a lot, and sometimes I smile when I think about playing with my BF at the half-a-house. I have special memories of my first best friend, even today....

Grits and Green Split Pea Soup

Ma had gone shopping. Daddy was home feeding us. Daddy put our bowls on the table and called us to come in and eat. We had had grits that morning, and there was some left over. Daddy put some cold grits in all the bowls.

We (my brothers, sister, and I) were sitting at the dinner table. We all stared at the cold grits in our bowls. Then we looked at each other. I know we were all thinking …. *MA!!!!!*

Daddy seemed quite pleased with himself as a chef. But he wasn't done yet. Next he grabbed each of our bowls, one at a time, and went into the kitchen. He brought back each bowl full of hot green-pea soup on top of those cold grits and ordered, "Eat!"

When I looked at my bowl of grits and soup, my eyes welled up with water. Ma never gave us food like this.

I looked at my brothers. Toogie was mad. His face was all scrunched up. My other brother was scared to say anything. My sister just looked away. She wasn't eating no grits, even if she had to sit there forever. Me—as usual, I started crying.

We sat there twisting and turning in our chairs. Daddy was no joke. He was head of his household, and, if we even *thought* of wasting food, we would be in big trouble. Wasting food was a "no-no." Everything on your plate had better be gone before you left the table (even if you hated what was on your plate) or you didn't leave the table. If we even looked like we were gonna complain, Daddy would backhand us … right out of our chair.

The soup got real cold, and Daddy was losing his patience with us. What could we do? We were terrified.

Suddenly we heard the front door open. "MA," I screamed! I saw my brothers' faces light up. Ma came into the dining room where we were sitting. She looked at our bowls. Her eyes got real big. "What's that?" she asked Daddy.

"What's what?" Daddy asked.

"What are they eating?" Ma asked Daddy.

"Food," said Daddy. "And they're gonna eat it!"

Ma gently and softly said to Daddy, "Now, William, they're not going to eat that. Maybe, if the grits were separate and hot or the soup was by itself, they'd eat it, but together … and cold—they'll sit there all day."

At that moment in our house, you could hear a pin drop. There was total silence as we held our breath. Then Daddy looked at Ma and said, "Well, all right, you all can go—but, until your Ma fixes dinner, you get nothing else."

We were hungry, but we tore off running from that table. Two chairs fell over as my brothers tried to beat each other out the room.

I ran and hugged Ma for saving us.

That evening, at dinnertime, we all sat together at the dinner table and ate everything on our plates.

(Of course, it was easier because Ma had made the meal!)

Happiness

Sheets of rain heavy with small bits of hail were pounding the living-room windows. It was a cold, dreary November day. I was feeling sort of lost and lonely as I looked out the window at the falling rain. For once, the house was quiet, but I could hear the howling wind rattling against the side of the house where the little mulberry tree's bare branches blew in the wind and freezing rain.

Within minutes, I heard the whining sound of the back door. Ma had just walked into the house, back home from the meat market and Raulston's grocery store.

The meat market and Raulston's were next to each other about three blocks away from our house.

I peeked at Ma as she was stamping her feet on the torn rubber doormat to try to get the rain water off her shoes. Ma took her purple wool coat off and shook it real hard. The water ran down the sides of her coat onto the floor. She hung her coat on the long brown skinny coat rack next to the little window in the corner of the room.

Ma looked around at the cold back room. My sister and brothers had left their muddy wet galoshes in the middle of the floor when they came home from school.

Two wet coats were on the floor, and one wet coat was on the washing machine. I knew that Ma was real mad when she saw that.

I quickly ran back into the room next to the kitchen and sat down on the wooden chair next to the door. Then Ma walked into the kitchen. When I peeked at Ma, I could tell she was very tired.

Ma slowly walked over to the icebox and, from the shelf, took out a bowl of neck bones that she had cooked the day before and put them in a pot on the stove. Ma had soaked some navy beans overnight, so she poured them into the pot with the neck bones.

"Joyyyce," she called, thinking I was upstairs. I said nothing. "JOYYYCE!" she yelled.

I quietly walked into the kitchen and looked at her. "Yes?" I asked.

I guess I startled Ma because her eyes got big and her head jerked back when she heard me. "You scared me! Did you hear me when I first called you?"

"Yes," I said softly.

"Why didn't you answer me when I called you?"

I shrugged my shoulders and looked at her.

Well, shrugging your shoulders at Ma was a BIG "no-no!" But Ma knew me well. She stared at me without another word. She knew I was feeling sad.

After considering the situation for a few minutes, Ma said, "Bring me that big black iron frying pan

so I can make some cornbread. Get the flour out of the cabinet."

I did. I put the flour on the table. It was heavy.

"Now bring me the buttermilk and eggs out of the icebox." (Back then we called our old beat-up refrigerator an "icebox.")

I got the buttermilk and eggs. I brought them to the table too.

Then Ma went to the top shelf of the cupboard next to the refrigerator and got some baking soda and salt. Ma opened the bottom cabinet door under the sink and pulled out a big jug of oil.

"Where's your brothers and sister," Ma asked?

"Upstairs. I think they're asleep" I said.

"Go wake them up and tell them I said to come clean up this mess they made in the back room. You help them get the water up and put their galoshes near the radiator to dry."

I went upstairs and woke up one of my brothers. My sister was in her room, so I just yelled to her.

"Ma said that y'all better go clean up the mess you made in the back room. It's all wet down there, and she's real mad," I told them both.

They both got mad at me because I was the messenger. I didn't care, I was mad too, because I always had to help Ma do the cooking and stuff while they did their homework. I was just a little girl.

They came downstairs and cleaned up the back room. By now, Ma had cut up a cabbage. She was frying that cabbage in a big pot on the stove. Boy, did it smell good! Then Ma started making the cornbread.

Ma mixed all that stuff together while we watched her. Then she put some oil in that big old black iron pan. The oil got real hot, and a little smoke came out of the pan.

"Move back away from the stove," Ma said as she poured a little of that hot oil in the batter and mixed it up. Then Ma poured the batter in that hot big black iron pan on the stove. The pan made a loud sizzling noise.

We had a gas stove with four burners and a grill on the stove. I remember watching Ma turn down the fire of the burner to medium low under the pan. Then Ma put a big lid on top of that frying pan.

Ma kept turning the pan in a circle every five or ten minutes to make sure the cornbread was cooked on all sides. When Ma took the top off the frying pan, she looked at the cornbread to see if there were holes or bubbles on the top of it.

When the cornbread was almost dry on top, Ma told me to go get her a big plate out of the dish cabinet. I did. She took the plate and ran cold water on it. Then Ma put the plate face down on the top of the cornbread.

Ma took a dishtowel, grabbed the handle of the frying pan and flipped that frying pan over. The cornbread plopped right out of that pan onto that wet plate. IT WAS GOLDEN BROWN AND BEAUTIFUL!!

Ma put the frying pan back on the fire on the stove. Then Ma gently slid the flipped cornbread off that wet plate back into the frying pan. She wanted to make sure the bottom side of the cornbread was cooked too.

Ma saw the delight in all our eyes when we saw the golden-brown cornbread.

To us, Ma was a hero! Now, nobody was mad.. "Set the table" she said. I got the forks; my brother got the plates and glasses.

Squeak …. *bang*… the back door swung open. A cold wind blew into the back room and the kitchen. "DADDY!" we yelled!

Daddy was a carpenter. He had been working on some houses in the area. Sometimes he worked at the air-force base too. Anyway, he was wet and grumpy. He looked at Ma, who was stirring up the cabbage. "Hi, DADDY!" we yelled. He looked at us and nodded as he took off his wet coat and hat.

"Dinner's ready," Ma said to Daddy. He nodded again and went to the bathroom to wash up.

Ma told my big sister to call my other brothers for dinner. They came running downstairs. We sat down at the dinner table, said the grace, and began fixing our plates. We began eating in silence ….

THE FOOD WAS SOOOOO GOOD!!! The house smelled so good. Daddy was quiet and pretty calm now. We were all together enjoying our dinner. We looked at Ma and smiled. She was our hero. She couldn't help smiling back at our beaming faces.

That day I learned a kind of mathematical equation: being together with my family while eating Ma's good homemade meal = happiness!

Ma's Top of the Stove Cast-Iron Cornbread

Ingredients

- 1 large egg (slightly beaten)
- ½ cup buttermilk
- ¾ cup milk
- ¾ cup all-purpose flour /sifted
- 1 teaspoon baking powder
- ½ teaspoon baking soda
- 1 teaspoon salt
- 1 ¾ cups yellow cornmeal
- 2 tablespoons vegetable oil

Utensils

- 2 medium-sized mixing bowls
- 1 7- to 9-inch cast-iron pan, with lid
- 1 full-size (8-inch) dinner plate

Directions

1. In the first bowl, sift together the flour, baking powder, baking soda, salt, and cornmeal.

2. Heat the cast-iron pan on low.

3. In the second bowl, mix together egg, buttermilk, and milk. Set aside.

4. Add the 2 tablespoons of oil to the pan. Increase heat to medium-high.

5. Add half the dry ingredients to the liquid ingredients. Mix lightly. Add the remaining dry ingredients and mix lightly.

6. When the oil in the pan is hot, carefully pour the cornbread mixture into the pan, which should sizzle.

7. After about three minutes (when the edges of the mixture appear slightly broken and crisp), turn the heat down to medium-low

8. Cover the pan. Grasping the pan handle with an oven mitt, slowly rotate the pan clockwise on the burner in a complete circle. Let it rest on the burner for two minutes, then repeat the process for about 20-30 minutes.

9. After 20 minutes, remove the lid and check the bread. If the mixture has dried out and the center is just about dry, it's time to increase the heat to medium-high and move to step 10.

10. Run cold water on the face of the dinner plate. Pour off excess water. Place the wet dinner plate face-down on

the cornbread. Using oven mitts, grab the handle of the pan and flip the cornbread onto the plate.

11. Place the pan back on the stove. Slide the flipped cornbread back into the pan so that the crisp brown bottom is now the top. Rotate for 10 minutes to complete the cooking process.

12. Remove from heat. Let sit for one minute. Slice and serve with butter.

Mmmmmmmmmm!

www.ingramcontent.com/pod-product-compliance
Lightning Source LLC
Chambersburg PA
CBHW041929040426
42444CB00018B/3468